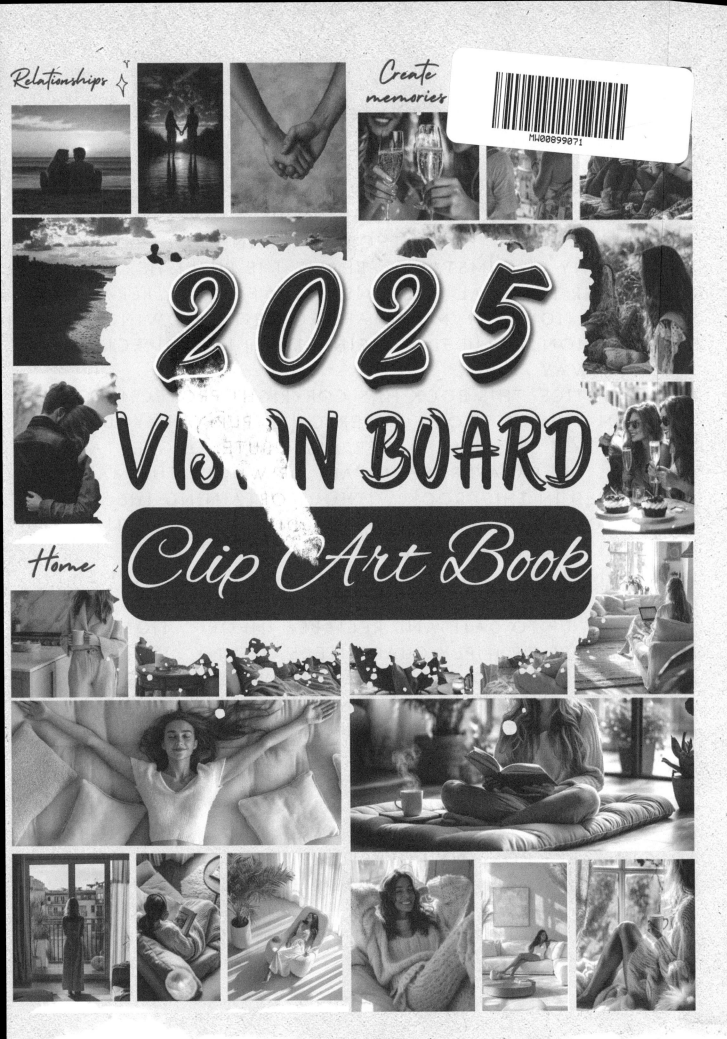

Relationships

Create memories

Home

# 2025
# VISION BOARD
## Clip Art Book

# Travel

# Explore

# Hobbies

# Stay creative ✧

*Spirituality* ✦

# faith

# Relationships

With Love & Respect

# Business

*Success* ✧

strategy

# SUCCESS
## *is a decision*

**Put** YOUR **ideas** OUT INTO THE WORLD

**Work HARD** SHOW THEM!

ready FOR BIGGER and BETTER things

# Home

# Quality
# Time

# friendships ✧

# Create
# memories

# family ✧

Strong together

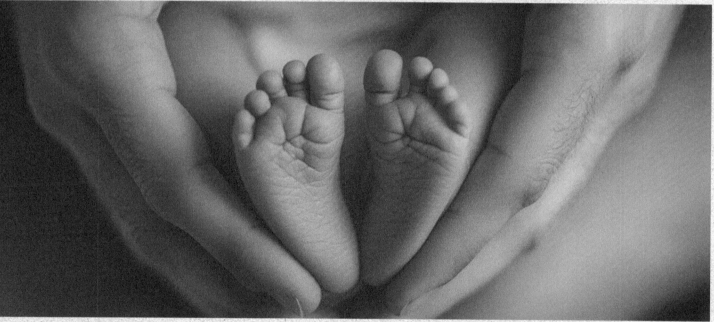

# Selfcare

# My Time ✦ ✧

# finance

Money

# Workout

I am motivated

# Healthy

I Love my Body

# Happiness ✧

# Wealth

# Dare to dream

# fashion

Positive Affirmations

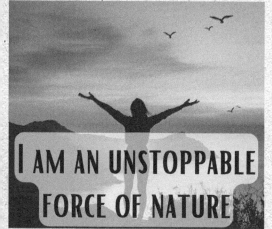
I AM AN UNSTOPPABLE FORCE OF NATURE

I AM SUCCESSFUL

I AM PURE, POSITIVE ENERGY

I AM A LIVING, BREATHING EXAMPLE OF MOTIVATION

I AM CONFIDENT

TODAY IS A PHENOMENAL DAY

ALL I NEED IS WITHIN ME RIGHT NOW

# Positive Affirmations

I USE OBSTACLES TO MOTIVATE ME TO LEARN AND GROW

I CAN BE WHATEVER I WANT TO BE

TODAY WILL BE A PRODUCTIVE DAY

AM GRATEFUL FOR EVERYTHING I HAVE IN MY LIFE

I AM INTELLIGENT AND FOCUSED

I AM LOVE, AND I AM LOVED

I FEEL MORE GRATEFUL EACH DAY

I AM ENOUGH. I HAVE ENOUGH

I PRIORITIZE MY WELL-BEING

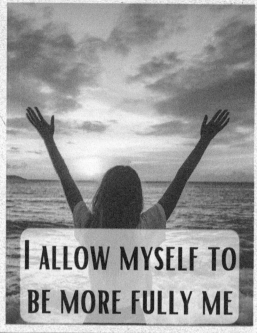

I ALLOW MYSELF TO BE MORE FULLY ME

EACH AND EVERY DAY, I AM GETTING CLOSER TO ACHIEVING MY GOALS

I AM HEALING AND STRENGTHENING EVERY DAY

I AM WORTHY OF WHAT I DESIRE

NOTE TO SELF: I AM GOING TO MAKE YOU SO PROUD

Positive Affirmations

I TRUST MYSELF TO MAKE THE RIGHT DECISIONS

I AM KIND TO MYSELF AND OTHERS

MY EFFORTS HELP ME SUCCEED

I TRUST MY INNER GUIDANCE AND FOLLOW IT

HAVE EVERYTHING I NEED TO ACHIEVE MY GOALS

I CAN MAKE A REAL DIFFERENCE

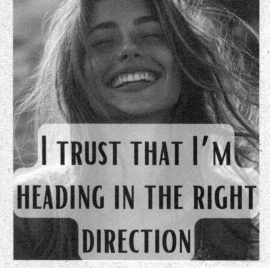

I TRUST THAT I'M HEADING IN THE RIGHT DIRECTION

*Positive Affirmations* ✧ ✧

**I AM GRATEFUL FOR WHAT I CAN DO**

**MY GOALS ARE ACHIEVABLE**

**I WILL BE KIND TO MYSELF TODAY**

**I HAVE FAITH IN MY ABILITIES**

**I DESERVE LOVE IN MY LIFE**

**I TRUST MYSELF**

**I AM ALWAYS LEARNING**

*Positive Affirmations* ✧ ✧

I AM POWERFUL

I WILL MAKE TIME FOR WHAT BRINGS ME JOY

I WILL ACCEPT MYSELF AS I AM

WILL TURN NEGATIVE THOUGHTS INTO POSITIVE ONES

I WILL TRY NEW THINGS

MY LIFE IS A GIFT

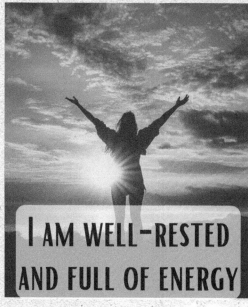

I AM WELL-RESTED AND FULL OF ENERGY

# Positive Affirmations

**I AM GROWING AT MY OWN PACE**

**MY MENTAL HEALTH IS A PRIORITY**

**I AM STRONG IN MIND, BODY, AND SPIRIT**

**I INHALE THE GOOD AND EXHALE THE BAD**

**I WILL FIND MOMENTS OF JOY TODAY**

**I EMBRACE MY POWER**

**I RADIATE LOVE AND POSITIVITY**

# *Thank you!*

We are absolutely delighted and deeply grateful for your recent purchase of our **Vision Board Clip Art Book**. Your support means so much to us, and we're thrilled for you to dive into the boundless creativity this book has to offer.

Creating a vision board is a powerful step toward manifesting your dreams and goals, and we designed this book to make the journey even more inspiring and visually captivating. With its vibrant illustrations and versatile elements, we hope it serves as a tool to help you craft a vision board that truly embodies your aspirations.

As you embark on your creative journey, we'd love to hear your feedback. Your insights are incredibly valuable—not only to us but also to others who might benefit from this resource. If you could take a moment to share your thoughts in an Amazon review, it would mean the world to us. Your honest feedback helps fellow dreamers discover how our **Vision Board Clip Art Book** can enhance their goal-setting journey.

Wishing you abundant inspiration and success as you bring your vision board to life!

Warm regards,
**ZAI Publishing**

## *Made with Love*

Made in the USA
Las Vegas, NV
22 December 2024

15248040R00044